WHERE THERE IS
SMOKE THERE IS DIRE

WHERE THERE IS SMOKE THERE IS DIRE

DIRE NEED TO QUIT PUFFING!

Brice Jacob

Writers Club Press
San Jose New York Lincoln Shanghai

Where There is Smoke There is Dire
Dire Need to Quit Puffing!

Writers Club Press
an imprint of iUniverse.com, Inc.

For information address:
iUniverse.com, Inc.
5220 S 16th, Ste. 200
Lincoln, NE 68512
www.iuniverse.com

ISBN: 0-595-15089-6

Printed in the United States of America

Preface

The following original rhymes are intended to motivate smokers to cease a habit that is destroying a human, today and tomorrow. These may also help to discourage beginning the habit at all. Smokers may view these rhymes as contemptuous or that they suggest a violation of their rights. Hopefully these rhymes add support to the intense widespread current campaign in the United States that discourages smoking. Stop-Look and see ill effects that are attributed to this addiction.

I dedicate these verses to those who successfully abdicate these curses, B.J.

9
DON'T DO IT !

Brice Jacob

1

Like murder 2nd. degree

Brice Jacob

2

Jack the man possessed a flair, For blowing smoke rings in the air, His polluting was thick, Co-workers got sick, Some were laid out flat, For them, that was that, And the same happened to that man Jack.

Brice Jacob

3

COMPREHEND

FRIEND

Brice Jacob

4

The warning appears on every pack, Proof for some it seems to lack, According to Tim, as he blew his smoke, All these claims are one big joke, But they laid him out flat. And that was that.

Brice Jacob

5

No laughing matter

Brice Jacob

6

To Kim the warnings were laughable, She inhaled far beyond her clavicle, Her lungs gave out, She lost the bout, They laid her out flat, And that was that.

Brice Jacob

7

Believe It And Kick It:

Brice Jacob

8

A two pack a day man was Jake,
Warnings and claims were all fake,
His thoughts would not bend,
He puffed to the end,
They laid him out flat,
And that was that,

Brice Jacob

9

Stay Strong

Not wrong.'

Brice Jacob

10

Ruby held her cig in her lips, She ignored all warnings and tips, The medics were wrong, She was so strong, But they laid her cut flat, And that was that.

Brice Jacob

11

SICK HICK

Brice Jacob

12

Elsis feared being a hick, Smoking for her was the trick, She posed, oh so cute, Blew smoke from her snoot, But they laid her out flat, And that was that.

Brice Jacob

13

BROKEN CRUTCH

Brice Jacob

14

Myrna only smoked a pack or two, Depending on what all she had to do, This was her crutch and no less, Made her lungs quite a mess, They laid her out flat, And that was that.

Brice Jacob

15

WILL POWER

Brice Jacob

16

Doc was long hooked on his smoking, He knew the medics weren't joking, Couldn't kick this old habit, Would have liked to dab nabitt, But they laid his out flat, And that was that.

Brice Jacob

17

Wheezy Easy

Brice Jacob

18

Toby was heard constantly wheezing, His throat seemed to be squeezing, He smoked them down short, Blew smoke with a snort, They laid him out flat, And that was that.

Brice Jacob

19

Sitting Duck

Brice Jacob

20

Jane smoked at home to unwind, Reviewing a hard day in her mind, She had smoked all day long, This her swan song, They laid her out flat, And that was that.

Brice Jacob

21

Don't do it unto others

Brice Jacob

22

Smoking for Ted was his thing,
What harm could this possibly bring?
Second-hand smoke,
To his spouse was no joke,
They laid her out flat,
And that was that,

Brice Jacob

23

The Kids
are.
Priceless

Brice Jacob

24

John's home strongly smells from his smoking,
A stench strong enough to cause choking,
The air there is bad,
For the kids it is sad,
Could lay then out flat,
Think of that

Brice Jacob

25

Chair is bare

Brice Jacob

26

Second-hand smoke got to Kile, He was able to survive a long while, No one seemed to care, About smoke in the air, Over there is his chair, They laid him out flat. And that was that.

Brice Jacob

27

Stones are
Anti-Sociable

Brice Jacob

28

Katy smoked to be sociable,
Warnings to her were Jokeable,
They laid her out prone,
Carved her name on a stone,
And that was that,

Brice Jacob

29

To the painful end.

Brice Jacob

30

Theo exclaimed while puffing, Everyone dies of something, Heart and lungs both gave out, Fought a long painful bout, They laid him out flat, And that was that.

Brice Jacob

31

Whisk the
Risk

Brice Jacob

32

Jessy is a wonderful fellow, His smoking seems so mellow, He is laid back and cool, Certainly nobodys fool, Listen up Jess, before your health is a mess, Quit while ahead, Don't rush to be dead.

Brice Jacob

33

Plant Good Seed

I

Brice Jacob

34

Tobacco is Billie's farm crop, The more we use it non-stop, Makes a long profitable trend, He will grow to the end, How many are flattened While his pockets are fattened?

Brice Jacob

35

Harvest

   a
Healthy Crop

Brice Jacob

36

LOOK at your tobacco farm,
How many lives can it harm?
Find a new use or new crop,
Encourage the smokers to stop,
Help create a new flair,
To inhale just plain fresh air,

Brice Jacob

37

Prediction

on

Addiction

Brice Jacob

38

Addiction to smoking is easy, At first a little bit queasy, But addiction will win, By puffing again and again, Many have proved that, And now are laid out flat.

Brice Jacob

39

Make laughs
   Last

Brice Jacob

40

Many will laugh at these rhymes, Snicker and shrug through the lines, But the record is clear, Many are no longer here, They laid then out flat, And that was that,

Brice Jacob

41

Curse The Worse

I

Brice Jacob

42

Smoking addiction a curse? health grows worse
and worse, Hauled away in a hearse, Laid out flat,
That is that.

Brice Jacob

43

Stinking Fantasy

Brice Jacob

44

Wish we had a chimney built in? Protruding somewhere through skin? Or maybe through hair, Blowing our smoke in the air, We would be built to blow smoke. Gee Whiz-okee-doak:

Brice Jacob

45

Protect A Voice

Brice Jacob

46

Theo drove and puffed his cigar, It smelled like crap in his car, His mouth became sore, Should have quit away before, No voice box anymore,

Brice Jacob

47

Up In Smoke

Brice Jacob

48

Bob lost his larynx too, He knew, He knew, He knew. No more smoking, Doc said, Bob would rather be dead, They laid him out flat. And Bob wanted that.

Brice Jacob

49

Lose
By
Hook or Crook

Brice Jacob

50

Jo enjoyed her smoking so much, Gave her a business-like touch, "I'll never get hooked". Warnings all overlooked, They laid her out flat, And that was that.

Brice Jacob

51

Can Do!

Forget to?

Brice Jacob

52

Many can quit anytime,
"The decision is totally mine,
It is no problem for me.
To be or not to be,
And now I am naught,
Smoking I'm not,
I am no longer coughin,
As I lay in my coffin"

Brice Jacob

53

Puff Strong

Not Far Long

Brice Jacob

54

A habit for either gender, Throats and lungs are so tender, Hearts may start out strong, But not last that long, Not nearly long enough, Weakened with every puff.

Brice Jacob

55

Break The
Chain

Brice Jacob

56

I

Reaching in pocket or purse, This is part of the curse, The motion to light, Daytime or night, Repeat and repeat and repeat, Eventually down in defeat.

Brice Jacob

57

By Example

Break It Off

Brice Jacob

58

Everyone in the family smokes, Greta is just one of the folks, Why not quit while ahead? Before all are dead.

Brice Jacob

59

Greatest Asset

Brice Jacob

60

Enjoy: BETTER HEALTH

KEENER SCENTS

TASTIER FOODS

MONEY SAVED

Brice Jacob

61

Think You Can

Brice Jacob

62

Quitting is very hard to do, The decision is up to you, You can do if you want to:

Brice Jacob

63

Make That Last One
The Last One

Brice Jacob

64

This is a good time to quit,
Get serious friend,
Don't let smoking Rush

65

The End

Brice Jacob

www.ingramcontent.com/pod-product-compliance
Lightning Source LLC
Chambersburg PA
CBHW031243280526
45784CB00004B/1695